GUIDE TO THE OLD LOGGERS PATH

THIRD EDITION

DAVE GANTZ

CATAMOUNT PRESS

an imprint of Sunbury Press, Inc.
Mechanicsburg, PA USA

For information about special discounts for bulk purchases, please contact Sunbury Press Orders Dept. at (855) 338-8359 or orders@sunburypress.com.

To request one of our authors for speaking engagements or book signings, please contact Sunbury Press Publicity Dept. at publicity@sunburypress.com.

FIRST CATAMOUNT PRESS EDITION: September 2025

Set in Adobe Garamond | Interior design by Crystal Devine | Cover by Lawrence Knorr | Edited by Debra Reynolds. All photos by the author.

Publisher's Cataloging-in-Publication Data
Names: Gantz, Dave, author.
Title: Guide to the Old Loggers Path / Dave Gantz.
Description: First trade paperback edition. | Mechanicsburg, PA : Catamount Press, 2025.
Summary: Featuring a ghost town, forgotten railroad grades, mountain views and beautiful streams including Rock Run, the nearly 28 mile Old Loggers Path is a great backpacking loop for beginner and experienced hikers. The Old Loggers Path Guide provides turn-by-turn instructions along with advice and information so hikers can enjoy and appreciate the trail and surrounding forest.
Identifiers: ISBN : 979-8-88819-319-8 (softcover).
Subjects: SPORTS & RECREATION / Hiking | TRAVEL / Northeast / Middle Atlantic (NJ, NJ, PA) | NATURE / Regional.

Designed in the USA
0 1 1 2 3 5 8 13 21 34 55

For the Love of Books!

TABLE OF CONTENTS

AUTHOR'S NOTE

My first time hiking the Old Loggers Path (OLP) was the winter of 2004-2005. I had directions to the trailhead in Masten and I knew if I followed the orange blazes, I would loop back to my car. The road to the forest was a sheet of ice, my camp stove didn't work, and I nearly ran out of food. However, I learned excellent backpacking lessons that weekend. Twenty years later, I am still visiting the trail at least annually to learn more about myself and the area. Why would I hike this same trail year after year? Besides the sheer love of hiking, I have also witnessed the forest changing.

The OLP is within the Pennsylvania Loyalsock State Forest. It is a forest of many animal species. Deer, bear, and porcupine are common. Step carefully, as rattlesnakes often den in rocky outcroppings and crevices. This forest also boasts excellent plants such as jewelweed, blackberry, blueberry, poison ivy, ramps, Indian cucumber root, mayapples, pitcher plant, marshmallow, and more. Predatory birds such as hawks, osprey, and eagles are abundant, as well as migratory songbirds. A short walk along any section of the OLP, with a keen eye, will provide plenty to see and learn.

The main route of the OLP generally meanders along old logging roads and railroads that were built over 130 years ago. At times, you can feel the old railroad ties under foot while walking on this now dirt trail. Iron tools and an old fruit orchard are easy to spot near Doe Run, and an old timber saw is a focal point on the trail near Krimm Road. The main trailhead parking area was a thriving lumber mill town for a few decades in the early 1900s. This area previously boasted railroads and several buildings to house members of the Civilian Conservation Corps. Now known as Masten Ghost Town, this once thriving community is a small forest campground where visitors can sleep on the remaining foundations of buildings.

The OLP leads through several stands of tree species and alongside several timber cuts. It can be disheartening to see the initial destruction, but visiting year after year has provided me with insight on how a forest can regenerate. Evidence of the regeneration can be felt by the stubbing of a toe on the shallow-rooted American beech on the trail. Striped maple often grow alongside the trail, while towering tulip poplar and black cherry provide plenty of shade in the hot summer months.

This forest is utilized for its other natural resources, too. Wind turbines on distant ridges, natural gas drilling sites, pipelines, and electric lines make a noticeable impact on the trail with noise and visual pollution that didn't exist decades ago. Destructive activities like these make lasting impacts on the ecology of the forest, and these effects and changes are noticeable after only a few visits.

Water is a major contributing factor to the look and feel of this area. In fact, some sections of trail and surrounding roads were decimated by major flooding events in the 2010s. It is remarkable to see the destruction caused by these powerful storms and floods. The southern section of the OLP, between Sharp Top Vista and Sprout Vista, provides a glimpse of how flood events reroute streams, erode mountains, and change the shape of the landscape altogether.

As far as I know, the trail itself has never been in better shape. Two backpacking shelters were built in 2017, and overall trail maintenance (nearly all volunteer) has been superb. Still, take a guidebook and some paper maps with you, because cell phone coverage is very limited in this forest. Always call Loyalsock State Forest while planning for the trip to ask for current conditions and updates. The main trail is well used and blazed. Unmaintained side trails and old logging grades are everywhere. For those who are comfortable and prepared to ramble through the woods without getting lost, go for it! Whatever you do, be sure to take some time to appreciate what was once here, what is here now, and how you can shape what will be here in the future for your children and grandchildren to experience.

I have been active in the outdoors my entire life, with my main passion being long distance hiking. My main goal in this work is to introduce and reconnect enthusiasts with the natural world. While this guidebook is not a completely comprehensive overview of the trail and forest, I hope to offer an accurate description of the trails so that more people can confidently explore this area, creating a desire to protect it. You can find more information regarding my hiking and backpacking adventures at: www.walkwithgantz.weebly.com.

DISCLAIMER

The author observed and measured the trail information presented in this guide in the spring of 2024. The author has spent time in this area through all four seasons, hiking the trail dozens of times since 2004, and has attempted to provide possible seasonal conditions throughout the guide. However, this trail lies on public forestland in the natural world and conditions are subject to change at any time. Because of this, all persons using this trail do so at their own risk. The author disclaims any and all liability for conditions along the trail, the accuracy of the data presented, hazards, and all material contained in this guide. All persons are encouraged to contact the Loyalsock State Forest (570.946.4049) regarding road and trail conditions before exploring the area. Also, please contact the author with any discrepancies for future updates to this guide.

ACKNOWLEDGMENTS

I would like to thank my friend and good hiking partner, Eriks Perkons. Eriks composed the text for the geology segment in this guide. Thanks to Kevin Busko for providing the measuring wheel that I used to collect data. I was fortunate enough to use *the* measuring wheel that trail legend Dr. Tom Thwaites used to mark out many footpaths in the state! More thanks to Scott Adams, who published and promoted the first two editions of this guidebook, and Crystal Devine, Lawrence Knorr, and Debra Reynolds from Sunbury Press for publishing this 3rd edition. Additional thanks go out to the PA Department of Conservation and Natural Resources (DCNR) for providing assistance and cooperation in creating and maintaining these trails. Several local volunteers, trail running groups, and Alpine Club of Williamsport organize events in order to maintain this wonderful trail and other trails throughout Pennsylvania—thanks to all of you. Most importantly, many thanks to my wife, Emily, for providing support and feedback for this updated edition.

ABOUT THE TRAIL AND FOREST

The Old Loggers Path (OLP) is a great walking path for beginner and experienced hikers alike. It was planned and developed in the late 1970s by John Eastlake, who at the time, was a forester for Pennsylvania. This looped trail explores the Loyalsock State Forest for nearly 28 miles. The trail climbs a total of 4,000 feet, meandering between 1,350 feet above sea level and 2,300 feet above sea level. It is fairly easy to access this state forest, which lies north of Williamsport, PA. There is plenty of water to be found year-round along most of the trail; in fact, your feet are guaranteed to get wet any day of the year. The main trailhead parking area is located in an old ghost town named Masten. The trail is used well enough and is frequently maintained by local volunteer trail users. While multiple side trails and old logging grades exist, these may not be maintained. Cell phone coverage is very limited in this forest.

One of Pennsylvania's most beautiful mountain streams, Rock Run, is considered by most to be the main highlight of the OLP. The trail meets Rock Run at the confluence of Yellow Dog Run (Yellow Dog Falls), then follows Rock Run upstream while climbing to the top of the plateau. Rock Run includes house-sized boulders and flumes, sculptured smooth from the rushing water. Upstream along Yellow Dog Run, near the trail, is another set of waterfalls. It is truly a magnificent area. Other highlights include: Masten Ghost Town, Sprout Point Vista, Sharp Top Vista, Rock Run Vista, and Sullivan Mountain.

The OLP generally follows old, yet gentle, logging roads and railroad grades. There are few steep climbs and descents, notably Sharp Top Vista and Sullivan Mountain.

The main trail is well marked with orange blazes. These blazes are approximately two inches wide and six inches tall and are painted on trees along the trail. The orange color indicates a hiking only trail. Other trails in the area may be marked with red blazes (indicating shared-use trails), blue blazes, or yellow blazes. Be sure to properly distinguish between the red and orange blazes at certain intersections! It can be easy to mistakenly follow the wrong-colored trail, which quickly becomes a very confusing and frustrating situation. On the OLP, arrows indicate turns in the trail, on side trails a double blaze, or two blazes painted vertically (one above the other), indicate a trail intersection or turn ahead. There are trail signs at some but not all trail intersections.

GEOLOGY

Eriks Perkons writes:

The landscape that the Old Loggers Path crosses is a product of the long and complex geologic history of Pennsylvania. The trail sits near the southern edge of the Allegheny Plateau, the geographic province that spans most of the northern and northwestern portion of the state. Immediately to the south lies the Valley and Ridge Province, notable for its long, parallel mountains and flat bottomed, fertile valleys. These linear features resulted from folding and faulting of sedimentary rock layers during the Allegheny orogeny, a period of mountain building caused by the slow collision of North America and Africa during the Carboniferous and Permian periods (325-260 million years ago). This folding deformed much of the eastern margin of North America and formed the core of today's Appalachian Mountains. Loyalsock State Forest sits just beyond the northwestern edge of this folding, where the Appalachians end and transition to the Allegheny Plateau. Here, the originally flat sedimentary layers are still roughly horizontal. Rivers and streams have since cut through these strata like a layer cake, forming the distinctive deep valleys and flat-topped plateaus seen today.

The rocks of the Old Loggers Path can be divided into four main groups: the Catskill Formation, the Huntley Mountain Formation, the Burgoon Sandstone, and the Pottsville Group, arranged from oldest to youngest (and bottom to top). The ages and brief descriptions can be seen on the accompanying geologic map.

The **Catskill Formation** formed on the western coast of an ancient mountain chain, where rivers flowing from the highlands met an ancient interior seaway and dropped their sediments in deltas and coastal marshes. These produce the relatively soft, fine-grained rocks underlying the entire area, but seen only in the southwest corner of the trail where

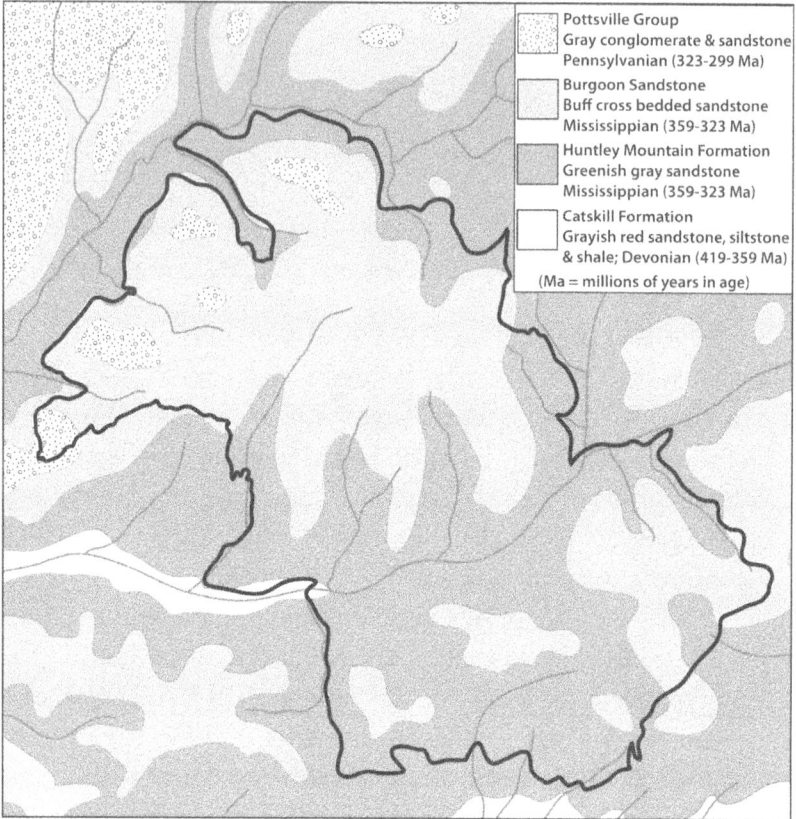

Pleasant Stream cuts completely through the overlying layers and exposes the Catskill rocks in the valley.

Above the Catskill Formation is the **Huntley Mountain Formation**, which most of the trail traverses. These rocks were likely formed after the coastline had migrated further west, and the rivers flowed across vast plains. Periodic floods would see the rivers spilling out onto the flat land, where they dropped fine grained sediments like fine sand, producing the greenish gray rocks seen today. This layer is best seen in the Rock Run area, where the fast-moving water has carved spectacular formations into the relatively easily eroded stone, or immediately west of Sharp Top Vista where the trail hugs a series of cliffs. These outcrops expose excellent cross bedding, which is the thin layering of the rocks seen when viewed from the side. These features result from ripples or small dunes migrating across the bottom of a flowing body of water. The thin layers of these cross beds were regionally quarried to produce flagstone (often inaccurately called "slate"), similar to what's seen along the old rail grade just north of Masten (around mile 27).

Many of the rocks that form the top of the plateau are part of the **Burgoon Sandstone**. This layer is more resistant to erosion than the underlying rocks, so it serves as a protective cap in areas where streams have not cut through and exposed the weaker lower units. These rocks were formed by streams flowing out of the growing mountains to the east, carrying and dropping coarser sands than the underlying Huntley Mountain Formation. With larger cross beds and sediments, the Burgoon typically breaks into blockier pieces than the Huntley Mountain, a habit visible in the large boulder piles near mile 3 (south of Masten).

Capping all of the layers locally is the **Pottsville Formation**. This layer is the most resistant to erosion of all, but has still been largely worn away after millions of years on the surface. The only portions of this unit remaining are found in the northwest area of the trail on Sullivan Mountain, above Rock Run. The large, gray rocks that provide many of the best views and ledges are comprised of this layer, such as at Big Rocks. The sediments forming these rocks were deposited closer to the ancestral Appalachians, which had by then started growing rapidly as Africa slowly collided to the southeast. The larger grains of sand and gravel indicate that the rivers and streams had not carried them as far from their place of origin.

It is also worth mentioning the strata that sit underneath all of this rock; even though they are deeply buried their presence has the chance to drastically alter the local landscape. Several layers down lies the Marcellus Shale, a thick body of black shale (a rock made of mud-sized sediments) deposited in the bottom of a deep sea. Deep waters are often low in oxygen, which generally makes it hard for organisms to live in these areas. Therefore, much of the organic debris (tiny dead things) that continually rains down from above escapes being eaten, and instead simply gets buried in the sediment. If buried deeply enough and exposed to the right temperatures and pressures, this organic material will convert to natural gas and oil. In 2008, a paper was published that massively raised the estimated amount of natural gas in the Marcellus Shale. While difficult to extract from shale, the quantity made it economically worthwhile to access via hydraulic fracturing, or "fracking." As companies race to extract this shale gas as quickly as possible, the Loyalsock Forest is at risk from the infrastructure and pollution associated with gas production. The Old Loggers Path is not likely to exist in its current state for very long before resource extraction degrades the natural beauty of the wilderness, with several active wells now visible just south of Sharp Top Vista. Get out and enjoy it while possible.

LOGISTICAL INFORMATION

Traditionally, most hikers begin their journey in Masten and hike in a counterclockwise direction. Many maps depict mileage in this manner, too. The author has hiked the trail multiple times in both directions and prefers to hike in a clockwise fashion. Hiking clockwise from Masten allows for a gentle first climb, when a backpacker's load is heaviest. Hiking clockwise also leaves the Rock Run area as a late and lasting impression of the trail. This stunning confluence of Yellow Dog Run and Rock Run is only 6.5 miles from the end of the hike.

There are several parking areas along the trail, which are noted in the trail description section. These include Masten Ghost Town, Yellow Dog Road, Ellenton Road, and Cascade Road. In addition, many established primitive campsites exist throughout the trail, as well as two-first come, first-served trail shelters, so hikers can be assured to find a camp spot no matter where they start or end their day. Hikers are encouraged to "hike your own hike" and explore the trail in whichever logistical manner that works best for personal wants and desires.

TRAIL MEASUREMENTS

The trail distances presented were originally measured with a steel wheel in 2014. The wheel measured metric units, which were converted to English units. The result was a 27.8-mile trail. These measurements should not be assumed as precise because there is a certain amount of human error involved (like when I was running off Sullivan Mountain in the midst of a lightning storm), but the wheel is the most consistent tool available. In 2020, and again in 2024, using my GPS watch to hike the trail and record new distances due to trail reroutes, the result with the GPS was a 27.2-mile trail in 2020 and a 27.0-mile trail in 2024. Quite honestly, every time I hike the OLP, I come up with slightly different data. I've kept the mileage presented in this guide at the original mark of 27.8 miles. It's safe to assume that a hiker will walk roughly 28 miles while hiking the OLP.

AVERAGE TIME NEEDED

Most hikers will need 2 to3 days to hike the entire 28-mile loop. However, with so many camping opportunities along the way, a hiker could enjoy several days on the trail. Ambitious hikers will attempt to walk the whole trail in one day: a daunting but achievable task. Long-distance trail runners sometimes realize that the loop is slightly longer than marathon distance and use the trail for training purposes!

ER CONTACT INFORMATION

UPMC Susquehanna is a regional hospital with an emergency room in Williamsport. It is approximately forty-five minutes to one hour from the trail. Contact information:

700 High Street
Williamsport, PA 17701
570.321.2850

It is paramount for every hiker to take proper safety precautions in this area. Bring a stocked first aid kit and know how to use it. Also, be sure to tell a family member or friend and the local foresters what your plans are and which direction you are hiking.

DIRECTIONS/PARKING

From Williamsport, PA: Head north on Route 15 towards Mansfield and Trout Run. Take the Trout Run/Canton/Route 14 North exit to the right and continue on Route 14 north for about 8.5 miles. Turn right on

Pleasant Stream Road. In 3 miles, turn left on Masten Road and follow this winding 6-mile forest road to Masten. This road was recently rebuilt, but it is still a gravel road and do beware, roads in Loyalsock State Forest are not maintained in the winter and can become extremely icy. After the enjoyable 9-mile drive into the forest, turn right before crossing the bridge at Masten. Head downhill to find the main trailhead parking. This parking area includes restrooms and car camping sites. Although free, these sites require reservations from the state forest (570.946.4049). This camping area can serve as an excellent basecamp for day hikers! There is also a backpacking site here for thru-hikers on the OLP.

IN THE EVENT THAT PLEASANT STREAM ROAD AND MASTEN ROAD ARE CLOSED

Continue another 3 miles north on Route 14 to reach the small community of Ralston. The second right hand turn is Thompson Street. Turn right onto Thompson Street and continue straight for two blocks. Follow Thompson Street as it turns left and then right, crossing a nice bridge over Lycoming Creek. The bottom of Rock Run is now on your right as the road turns to a gravel surface.

After entering the forest, stay right at a Y intersection. This is now Rock Run Road. Continue straight for about 3.5 miles. Notice the many day-use parking lots along the sides of the road. The cool air and cold water in Rock Run Valley make for a very popular destination during those hot summer days of July and August. Across the stream is Sullivan Mountain (the OLP walks along the top of this mountain, overlooking Rock Run). Soon the road will turn right and cross a bridge over the stream. There is parking on either side of this bridge, and an unmarked trail that leads east to the OLP at the confluence of Yellow Dog Run and Rock Run. Continuing on the road, now called Yellow Dog Road, climb the mountain for just over 2 miles, with Yellow Dog Run flowing on the left. There is a small OLP parking lot where the trail crosses Yellow Dog Road. Shortly thereafter, reach a T intersection and turn left onto Ellenton Ridge Road. Follow this road for about 3 miles. Along the way is another OLP parking area to the right on Krimm Road (notice the orange blazes along the roadway). This is a large parking area, and a great spot to begin or end a hike. Soon after, pass a natural gas industrial area on private property and make a hard turn to the right onto Masten road. Follow this downhill, about 1.5 miles to the ghost town of Masten. The main trailhead parking area is to the right, down a short hill.

OTHER RESOURCES

Tom Thwaites: *50 Hikes in Central PA* (2001)
Jeff Mitchell: *Backpacking Pennsylvania*
Purple Lizard Maps: Loyalsock-Worlds End Lizard Map

CAMPING INFORMATION

There are many campsites located throughout this path and two trail shelters. I have listed almost all of the established sites that I noticed from the trail. Of course, there is ample opportunity for hikers to wander further off the trail to enjoy a remote, peaceful night in the woods, as well. All hikers must follow Leave No Trace principles, which are discussed in the following pages. Hikers do not need a permit to camp in Loyalsock State Forest unless they plan to stay in one spot for more than one night. Campsites must be at least 100 feet from any water source and at least 25 feet from any trail. Call Loyalsock State Forest (570.946.4049) for more information on any other regulations that the hiker needs to follow.

WATER

There is generally plenty of water to be found along this trail. In fact, there can be too much water along the trail during wet seasons! There are many bridgeless stream crossings. One crossing, Pleasant Stream, is typically knee deep, and can be dangerous in high water (waist deep or more).

Hikers should always be prepared to treat any water that is obtained in the forest. Waterborne illnesses can live in the water, so it should be boiled, filtered, or chemically treated before being used. Don't be fooled though, water sources can and will go dry during droughts. Always call Loyalsock State Forest beforehand to ask for current conditions and updates.

FIRE

Fires are allowed most times of year. Fires are banned from March 1 to May 25 and other times when the fire danger is posted as High, Very High, or Extreme. During these times, the forest is actually considered to be in a dry season. Dry, dead leaves on the forest floor during these seasons will easily ignite to start forest fires. Please keep all fires contained in a fire ring. Always have plenty of water nearby and be sure that any fire is out completely before leaving it unattended.

FLORA AND FAUNA

There are a plethora of plant and animal species to experience along the OLP. A hiker will walk through hardwood forests as well as sections of pine and hemlock trees. Dozens of wetland plant species exist throughout the trail. Highlights include flowering plants, ferns, moss, fungus and edible berries. There are also plants that hikers generally despise like nettles, briars, and invasive barberry.

I have seen plenty of porcupine along this trail. The most popular spot I've noticed is along the upper regions of Rock Run. These peaceful herbivores will not bother you as long as you don't touch or step on them! The same rules apply for rattlesnakes. There are active den and rookery (nesting) rattlesnake sites in this forest and along this trail. Please treat rattlesnakes, as all creatures of the forest, with the utmost respect. Do not encroach upon their territory, as this can be perceived as a threat. Bear, coyote, and other mammals also live in PA forests. Luckily, none of these animals prey on humans. They may try to enjoy your food though, so be sure to practice Leave No Trace principles and secure your food away from your campsite and out of reach of any forest inhabitants.

Many hikers agree that the greatest human threat in PA forests is a small parasite: the tick. Be sure to take proper precautions to mitigate exposure and risks of tick bites while exploring in Pennsylvania!

HUNTING

Hunting is allowed in Pennsylvania State Forests and along the OLP. During hunting seasons, please wear a blaze orange hat and shirt at all times; and be respectful towards hunters. Not all hunters are required to wear orange, so be sure that they can see you even if you can't see them! The most popular hunting seasons in Pennsylvania occur during the months of September through January, and April through May.

LEAVE NO TRACE

Leave No Trace Outdoor principles embrace the idea of leaving the forest just as you found it. Take only pictures; leave only footprints. The seven principles are:

1. Plan ahead and prepare
2. Travel and camp on durable surfaces
3. Dispose of waste properly
4. Leave what you find
5. Minimize campfire impacts
6. Respect Wildlife
7. Be considerate of other visitors

Please do your part by following the above guidelines.

GUIDE TO THE OLD LOGGERS PATH

27.8 Miles
Clockwise from Pleasant Stream Bridge at Masten:

MI Clockwise	TRAIL DESCRIPTION	MI Counter Clockwise
0.0	Begin at the west end of the bridge on Upper Pleasant Stream Road, Masten. Approximate elevation at the start of the trail is 1,550 feet above sea level. Cross a bridge over North Pleasant Stream and continue on the gravel roadway. There is a backpacking campsite, restrooms, and car camping sites (reservations required, 570.946.4049) downstream on the west side of the bridge, across from the main trailhead parking area.	27.84
0.31	Cross a new stone sided bridge over Pleasant Stream and continue straight. Soon, turn left along Upper Pleasant Stream Road; Mill Creek Road leads to the right. Take note of the extreme flood damage caused by flooding in 2016. An overflow parking area is expected to be built here in the 2020s.	27.53
0.48	The trail turns right off the road, onto a single-track trail.	27.36
0.53	Trail register. Please sign in. These registers help maintainers and state foresters to know how many visitors use the trail. Registers are also used to locate a hiker in an emergency situation. Take note of the old rail grade leading west just past this register. This leads shortly back to Mill Creek Road, crosses the road, and then continues to follow the railroad grade Susquehanna and New York Railroad Trail (S&NY RR Trail)	27.31

MI Clockwise	TRAIL DESCRIPTION	MI Counter Clockwise
(cont.)	along the southside of Pleasant Stream for roughly 3 miles until it reconnects with OLP at mile 10.24. This trail, if blazed and maintained, can be a great cutoff option for those looking to hike the southern half of OLP, and for times when Pleasant Stream is too high to cross at mile 10.38.	
0.58	A stream, Bear Run, runs under the trail. Look for a possible campsite upstream along Bear Run. While there is an unmarked trail to the right, please stay on the marked path, which leads gently uphill along various logging grades. The trail will climb about 500 feet in the next 3 miles and eventually lead just past the headwaters of Bear Run.	27.26
0.98	Trail crosses a seasonal side stream. Notice plenty of poison ivy and jewelweed along this old path. Take note of the remains of coal along the treadway here. The OLP is following an old railroad grade.	26.86
1.06	The trail takes a switchback to the right. Continue to climb on the logging grade.	26.78
1.55	Notice the young forest overtaking the edges of this logging grade. Young white birch trees and American beech trees line the path. Unfortunately for the hiker, birch and beech trees have shallow root systems. These are the roots that hikers stumble over in this section of trail.	26.29
2.06	Cross seasonal side stream.	25.78
2.13	Cross seasonal side stream.	25.71
2.55	Another muddy crossing during wet weather. Ahead, the trail goes through several thick sections of mountain laurel, the PA state flower. Mountain laurel is a beautiful flower that blooms throughout this forest in June. Similar to rhododendron, the leaves of mountain laurel are smaller than rhododendron.	25.29

MI Clockwise	TRAIL DESCRIPTION	MI Counter Clockwise
2.64	Notice a campsite across the stream.	25.20
2.92	Reach an open canopy section of the woods. Shortly, the trail turns right.	24.92
3.14	The trail curves to the right again.	24.70
3.26	A younger hardwood forest prevails, saplings abound.	24.58
3.50	Begin a gentle descent of about 150 feet. Indian cucumber-root plants can be found in this area.	24.34
3.60	The trail crosses a grassy double-track and re-enters the woods and continues downhill.	24.24
3.73	A few possible campsites line both sides of the trail just before reaching a gravel road, Mill Creek Road. Do beware, this is a wet area, so plenty of mosquitoes and other biting insects may abound here during the spring and summer months. The trail turns left on Mill Creek Road to cross the stream culvert, then turns right off of the road and onto a forest driveway.	24.11
3.78	The trail turns right onto the signed 'Old Proctor Road Trail'.	24.06
3.92	A perpetually muddy area here. The trail continues straight and begins to ascend slightly to regain the plateau.	23.92
4.14	Climb through an open canopy forest that allows plenty of light for the fern undergrowth.	23.7
4.23	Notice a fire ring and a small space for sleeping to the left of the trail, just before crossing an unnamed gravel double-track road. There is a deer fence erected to the right a few hundred meters to the right along the road. History buffs will be interested in turning left along this road, which leads to Sprout Point. Sprout Point is the site of an old forest fire tower and stone building (the fire tower is long gone).	23.61

MI Clockwise	TRAIL DESCRIPTION	MI Counter Clockwise
4.37	After a quick descent, the trail leads through a wet area with the first real showing of nettle (stinging nettle or wood nettle) on this trail. Stinging nettle and wood nettle are two similar plants; both seem to 'bite' a hiker who brushes against them. The burning sensation goes away, usually after several minutes, so it's not that bad. Until it is that bad! Nettle is found in moist areas, oftentimes along mountain streams. There is a lot of nettle on the OLP!	23.47
4.69	Pass by blackberry bushes along the trail. In season (July-August), these delicious berries are enjoyed by hikers, black bears, and other forest critters.	23.15
4.83	The trail now turns right and continues to descend. To the left is a yellow blazed side trail. This trail leads 0.1 miles to Sprout Point Vista and a three-sided trail shelter. The shelter is an 'Adirondack' shelter—similar to those found on the Appalachian Trail. Sprout Point vista provides a great view south to many valleys and ridges, and the nearby shelter provides room to sleep for 6-8 hikers. There is also enough room nearby for two tents. Water can be found along the headwaters of East Branch Wallis Run, just off the main OLP in the drainage near the trail. Here, the stream is seasonal at best; hikers may have to walk downstream to find adequate water. Cell service reported here.	23.01
4.86	Turn left and descend. The trail descends about 500 feet in the next mile.	22.98
5.02	Stinging nettle again overgrows the old roadbed, in summer months, in this area. Notice the very large ash, hickory, and tulip poplar forest. Most of the ash trees in this forest are dead or dying due to the Emerald Ash Borer beetle.	22.82
5.03	Trail turns right. Just behind and above the hiker, about 150 feet up a steep mountainside, is Sprout Point Vista and shelter area.	22.81

MI Clockwise	TRAIL DESCRIPTION	MI Counter Clockwise
5.18	Switchback to the left. More nettle; the water source rarely flows here.	22.66
5.39	The trail turns right near a fire ring and possible campsite. The water flows seasonally here.	22.45
5.65	Notice the young tulip poplar trees and striped maple trees along the trail. Tulip poplar trees grow straight and fast and tall. In the spring, the flowers emerge and somewhat resemble tulip flowers. The striped maple tree also grows fast but can become top heavy and bent over. The bark looks to have vertical 'stripes' or 'scratch marks'.	22.19
5.75	Travel directly across a gravel road, Cascade Road, and continue into the woods. There is parking here, room for about 6-8 vehicles. Shortly, the trail turns right and approaches a trail register. Trail registers are a good place to let trail maintainers know of trail issues. These registers also help to locate a lost hiker and track the number of users on each trail. Please sign in and thank the volunteers who make this trail possible!	22.09
5.85	Cross East Branch Wallis Run, which is still a seasonal stream at this elevation. Take note of the massive damage caused to these drainages from multiple flooding events the last several years. These mountain streams eventually drain into Wallis Run, which is a significant tributary to Loyalsock Creek.	21.99
5.87	The trail turns left onto what appears to be an old road. A fire ring and campsite lie to the right.	21.97
5.97	Turn right off this old roadbed. Another fire ring and campsite lie straight ahead.	21.87
6.05	Small stream crossing.	21.79
6.33	Notice a small, unused campsite to the left of the trail, under hemlock trees.	21.51

MI Clockwise	TRAIL DESCRIPTION	MI Counter Clockwise
6.49	Cross two more seasonal streams. There is a campsite to the right just after these crossings.	21.35
6.51	Turn left and begin to ascend. Now enter a logging area. Although it may feel as though this trail is in the middle of absolutely nowhere, Loyalsock Forest is in fact a heavily managed forest. This area was logged before 2020 but is already regenerating. Take note of the trees that were not cut in this area—black cherry trees—these trees are highly valuable for many forest animal species and humans alike.	21.33
6.61	Streambed that is often dry.	21.23
7.00	As the trail follows the contour of the mountain, it crosses more seasonal streams.	20.84
7.08	Notice the nice campsites on the west side of this stream crossing. There used to be a campsite on the east side as well, but the stream rerouted itself during the flooding of 2016; now it leads directly over the old fire ring for this campsite. This mountain tributary is reliable year-round.	20.76
7.25	The trail turns right and begins the 600-foot ascent to Sharp Top Vista. The climb quickly becomes drier and steeper.	20.59
7.52	Oak trees.	20.32
7.67	To the left is a wet area that may have a spot for camping; but it also has a lot of stinging nettle.	20.17
7.80	Turn left to climb a very steep section of trail.	20.04
7.83	Cross a seasonal stream (usually dry). Trail begins a short but extremely steep climb here!	20.01
7.98	At a left turn the trail levels for just a bit, take note of the dry campsite here.	19.86
8.02	Trail turns right and begins the final push to the top.	19.82

MI Clockwise	TRAIL DESCRIPTION	MI Counter Clockwise
8.21	Reach John Merrell Road. To the left along the road is Sharp Top Vista. This is a spectacular vista looking south towards Williamsport! The vista includes a picnic table and panoramic views of the valley below. Camping is prohibited here, but long lunch breaks are encouraged. Take note of the large number of sumac trees growing just below the vista. These trees usually bloom in June and July. Fans of staghorn sumac can make pink lemonade from this shrub.	19.63
8.44	The trail leaves the road and follows a single-track trail to the left.	19.40
8.70	The trail hugs the edge of a series of cliffs, often immediately above or below well-exposed rock. These rock outcroppings are fun to observe, and a nice addition to this trail. Amateur geologists may be interested in this statement from Eriks Perkons: While existing geologic maps identify these rocks as belonging to the Huntley Mountain Formation, the color and excellent cross bedding lead to their tentative assignment as part of the Burgoon Sandstone. Cross bedding is the thin layering of the rocks that is visible when viewed from the side. These features result from ripples or small dunes migrating across the bottom of a flowing body of water.	19.14
8.79	The trail crosses a gravel road, which has been utilized for logging operations in the recent past. There are several downed trees on the opposite side of the road—look for the orange blazes to find the OLP on the other side of the road.	19.05
8.89	Descend. OLP descends 700 feet in the next 1.5 miles along Butternut Run. Although the trail rarely gets close to this mountain stream, it is often audible from the trail and an impressive site for hikers who venture off trail to explore the area. There are more patches of blackberry bushes along the trail here.	18.95

MI Clockwise	TRAIL DESCRIPTION	MI Counter Clockwise
9.00	Jewelweed is noticeable along this descent. The trail is also quite wet most times of year.	18.84
9.22	It now becomes more obvious that the trail is following an old logging grade. Continue to descend on a nice, but often wet, trail.	18.62
9.56	Butternut Run is reliable year-round at this point. The trail follows near this stream until it joins with Pleasant Stream.	18.28
9.70	Cross several seasonal side streams, up to 15, over the next section.	18.14
10.24	Reach a stand of young hemlock trees to the left. To the right, take note of the yellow blazed S & NY RR Trail. This trail follows along the southside of Pleasant Stream for roughly 3 miles until it reconnects with OLP at mile 0.53. It may be a great cutoff option for those looking to hike the southern half of OLP and for times when Pleasant Stream is too high to cross.	17.60
10.38	Notice a large campsite to the right, just before the trail crosses Pleasant Stream. Also take note of the extreme amount of damage in this area due to recent flooding events! This stream crossing can be high and swift any time of year. It can be especially hazardous in early spring, as the snow melts from the mountains.	17.46
10.43	A few campsites can be found on the opposite side of the stream.	17.41
10.47	Reach a T-intersection. Previously the OLP went left, but now it leads right on a new and most likely permanent reroute. Soon, the trail will begin to ascend as it gains over 700 feet in the next 3 miles to regain the plateau.	17.37

MI Clockwise	TRAIL DESCRIPTION	MI Counter Clockwise
10.54	The trail is now parallel with, but not directly beside Short Run as it heads upstream, crosses the old abandoned Pleasant Stream Road, and leads to the new Masten Road. Cross Masten Road, then follow the blazes as they lead left along an old grade.	17.30
10.97	Reach another old grade and follow the blazes as they lead right. To the left is the old trail, which quickly leads back to Masten Road.	16.87
11.43	OLP continues to follow this grade, to head west toward Long Run before turning north and ascending near, but always above, Long Run.	16.41
11.83	Notice the campsite below. This site is along the old OLP route, which is blazed yellow and leads back to a parking area on Masten Road. Continue straight, upstream, along the grade.	16.01
12.20	Cross a drainage, which usually makes for a wet trail.	15.64
12.37	OLP turns left and descends to Long Run.	15.47
12.45	Just before crossing, you may notice the unblazed Long Run Trail that continues straight, upstream and uphill, sometimes steeply, until it eventually reaches Cherry Ridge Trail and eventually Ellenton Ridge Road. Thank your local volunteer trail runners for reopening this wonderful trail.	15.39
12.49	Cross Long Run. There is a campsite directly on the trail (not recommended), and one campsite a few yards upstream. This is the last reliable spot to resupply water until 16.06 miles.	15.35
12.55	As the climb begins with a few switchbacks, notice a better campsite near the stream to the right.	15.29
13.24	The trail becomes steep towards the top.	14.60
13.40	A dry campsite can be found on the level area near the top of Sullivan Mountain.	14.44

MI Clockwise	TRAIL DESCRIPTION	MI Counter Clockwise
13.73	The trail meanders up and down for a bit as it leads along the top of the mountain. Rock formations can be seen all around the top of this mountain.	14.11
13.83	Gas pipeline crosses trail. This pipeline will cross the trail 3 more times.	14.01
13.89	Begin gentle descent. Notice the large, old hemlock tree to the left of the trail.	13.95
14.01	The trail becomes very wide; some areas of the forest appear to have been disturbed by large machinery related to the natural gas industry.	13.83
14.36	A disappearing double-track path appears on the left. This was never marked on official maps and suddenly appeared during the mid 2010s when the natural gas industry was scouring the land for possible drilling sites. The trail stays straight.	13.48
14.56	The OLP turns left at double blazes, near a large hemlock tree, and begins uphill. The path straight ahead at this intersection is known as the Crandall Road Trail. This trail rejoins the Old Loggers Path at 15.94 miles and can be used as a cutoff if necessary.	13.28
14.70	The trail becomes steeper and utilizes a few switch-backs to regain the top of the mountain.	13.14
14.80	The reward for this climb is to the left. A nice rock outcrop offers views to the east.	13.04
15.01	Another nice vista along the trail as it meanders through rocks on the edge of the mountain. When I was last here, I spotted 7 rattlesnakes, all black phase, staying warm on the rocks. These snakes were most likely pregnant females, who spend the whole summer together in a sort of 'rookery' while incubating their young. Rattlesnakes are a protected species, which offers Pennsylvania yet another reason to not turn this area into an industrial zone. Please do not disturb or harm these snakes in any way.	12.83

MI Clockwise	TRAIL DESCRIPTION	MI Counter Clockwise
15.44	The trail encounters another rock vista. Directly below the vista, deep in the valley is Middle Falls of Rock Run. Wind turbines can be seen across the valley on the adjacent ridge tops.	12.40
15.69	The trail drops off of this plateau via a short, steep, and rocky descent.	12.15
15.76	Turn right on a grassy path.	12.08
15.94	Trail crosses the other end of Crandall Road Trail, to the right, which leads back to the OLP at mile 14.56. The OLP stays straight on a grassy path. This path is Ellenton Grade, which is a gated extension of Ellenton Ridge Road. Hikers in need of an emergency cutoff can follow this path/road eastbound about 2 miles to Yellow Dog Road.	11.90
16.06	Cross stream, Buck Run, which (surprisingly) usually has running water. Buck Run drains into Rock Run just above Middle Falls. This is a favorite spot of mine. Trail immediately turns left off of the road. Notice a campsite on the right.	11.78
16.31	Cross a number of seasonal streams that flow into Buck Run and Rock Run. This section of trail is fast and relatively easy, but don't forget to look around and enjoy the forest!	11.53
16.96	Notice the old iron machinery parts that were left from past times.	10.88
17.03	This old logging road splits. The OLP heads towards the left, downhill, and becomes a very gentle and open road with many seasonal stream crossings.	10.81
17.52	The trail turns right and heads upstream shortly along Doe Run. Notice a nice, small campsite below the trail to the left and a large campsite above the trail to the right. Also take note of the fairly new trail shelter	10.32

MI Clockwise	TRAIL DESCRIPTION	MI Counter Clockwise
(cont.)	just before crossing Doe Run. This shelter is an 'Adirondack' shelter—similar to those found on the Appalachian Trail.	
17.59	Cross Doe Run. The trail turns to the left after crossing the stream and immediately heads back downstream. Doe Run Trail, on the other hand, leads upstream to Ellenton Grade.	10.25
17.71	Another nice campsite can be found to the right of the trail. The tread way continues downhill for a short spell.	10.13
17.75	Trail turns right onto another level, but rocky logging grade. As usual on the OLP, plan to encounter several seasonal side streams.	10.09
18.18	Notice a clearing to the right. Look closer to notice several old fruit trees in this clearing. Was this an old homestead?	9.66
18.26	In the wet season, there will be loads of club moss species to the left of the trail.	9.58
18.70	A yellow-blazed side trail leads to Rock Run Vista. This is a great view of Rock Run directly below, and McIntyre Wild Area directly across from the Rock Run drainage.	9.14
19.07	Cross the gas pipeline for a second time.	8.77
19.39	Notice Yellow Dog Run Road below the trail to the left. Shortly, the trail will meet with this gravel road.	8.45
19.59	Trail register. Please sign in.	8.25
19.63	Reach Yellow Dog Run Road. There is enough roadside parking here for 2-4 cars, but better parking is just ahead at mile 19.90. The trail turns right along the road for a bit.	8.21

MI Clockwise	TRAIL DESCRIPTION	MI Counter Clockwise
19.83	OLP turns left off of the road onto a trail. Soon enough the trail will begin its 600-foot descent to Rock Run.	8.01
19.90	Cross the top of Yellow Dog Run and notice a campsite on the right. A yellow-blazed trail leads to the right on a short path to Yellow Dog Road Parking Area.	7.94
20.03	Now the trail joins an old logging grade and begins to descend. Near here, Yellow Dog Trail, which may or may not be blazed, makes a hard right to lead south and uphill back to Ellenton Ridge Road. This trail, which is an old grade, leads past a marshy area with plenty of great wetland plant species.	7.81
20.20	Cross a branch of Yellow Dog Run, which feeds into the main branch of Yellow Dog Run. Continue to descend on the logging grade.	7.64
20.63	Yellow Dog Run can be heard and seen here. It is a beautiful stream, although the trail ahead can easily become washed out after heavy rains.	7.21
20.79	Notice the wonderful waterfalls on Yellow Dog Run. Take time to hike a bit off trail to visit these waterfalls.	7.05
21.00	Cross the gas pipeline for the third time.	6.84
21.33	Reach the confluence of Yellow Dog Run and Rock Run. There are several campsites at this spot. Rock Run is especially gorgeous here. An unblazed side trail leads across the top of Yellow Dog Falls, then downstream along Rock Run to Yellow Dog Road. This is sometimes referred to as the 'Yellow Dog Falls Shortcut Trail.' The popularity of this area and Rock Run Valley in general, will most likely lead to the closure of overnight camping here in the near future. Please enjoy this area with the utmost respect to the natural resources. The OLP turns right, heading upstream along Rock Run.	6.51

MI Clockwise	TRAIL DESCRIPTION	MI Counter Clockwise
21.50	Off to the left of the trail, Hawk Run splashes into Rock Run with a 50-foot waterfall. It's worth taking a peek at this beautiful spot.	6.34
21.59	Cross a small side stream that flows under a stand of hemlock trees. The OLP will generally side hill upstream above Rock Run for the next couple of miles. Overall, the trail climbs over 700 feet back to the top of the plateau.	6.25
21.71	Turn right, uphill, at a campsite, just after crossing the gas pipeline for the fourth and final time. Another campsite exists even further upstream.	6.13
22.06	The trail turns towards the left.	5.78
23.00	As the trail climbs up and away from the Rock Run drainage, notice how the ecosystem changes from hemlocks to hardwood species such as cherry, birch, beech, oak, maple, and others. When the trail drops down towards cool moist areas again, the hemlock will reappear. In addition, take note of sections of forest heavy with ferns, and other sections heavy with club moss.	4.84
23.17	Cross a seasonal stream, often dry, and climb steeply to a logging grade.	4.67
23.90	Cross the top of a seasonal stream that flows into Rock Run. A small campsite exists here.	3.94
24.02	Here the trail quickly descends to cross a waterway and then quickly ascends back to the grade. There is a nice campsite here. Also, a yellow blazed trail, Sharp Shinned Trail, turns to the left. This trail leads downstream to Rock Run, then back uphill to rejoin OLP at 24.77 miles. Do beware, this trail has been removed from the official DCNR maps, so although it is still blazed, it is probably not maintained and could be in poor condition.	3.82

MI Clockwise	TRAIL DESCRIPTION	MI Counter Clockwise
24.30	The trail now levels and widens. Here, you may notice noise pollution from natural gas activity upstream.	3.54
24.70	Cross yet another wet area. I often see porcupine along this section of trail.	3.14
24.77	On the left is a yellow double blaze trail and sign that indicates the Sharp Shinned Trail, which leads downstream to Rock Run. Sharp Shinned Trail then connects with Hawkeye Ski Trail on the north side of Rock Run. The OLP here, on the other hand, continues straight.	3.07
24.97	A large number of young striped maple trees cover the forest.	2.87
25.20	Notice the deer fence to the left of the trail. Deer fences are usually erected to deter deer from eating young trees; which helps to ensure the growth of saplings into mature trees.	2.64
25.33	The trail now makes a sharp right onto a dirt double-track. This section of trail used to be extremely muddy. Then it was filled with oversized gravel and the drainage system was updated. Now, it is a relatively easy, dry walk along a forest road.	2.51
25.48	Look for a quick left onto a single-track trail that is quite steep and washed out from rain runoff. The climb does not last too long, though. To the left of the trail is private property, and recent natural gas industry work.	2.36
25.66	The trail reaches a gravel road, Ellenton Ridge Road, and turns left.	2.18
25.70	The trail now turns right onto another gravel road, Krimm Road. Soon, the trail leads past a parking area and a gate in the road. Notice another deer fence on the right of this road. Nearby Natural Gas activity and a quarry on private land can cause quite a bit of noise pollution in this section of forest and the trail.	2.14

MI Clockwise	TRAIL DESCRIPTION	MI Counter Clockwise
25.76	A blue blazed trail, Cherry Ridge Trail, leads to the right. This trail also continues straight, running in conjunction with the OLP. The Cherry Ridge Trail is a 5.7-mile loop that remains on the plateau and skirts above Long Run, Short Run, and Bovier Run. The OLP continues straight.	2.08
26.07	The Old Loggers Path now turns left, off the road. Don't miss this turn! There is a trail register near an old saw. Notice the inscription on the saw, "The Old Loggers Path."	1.77
26.34	As the trail turns sharply to the left it also begins a steep descent. The trail will drop nearly 600 feet in less than 2 miles. This is the beginning of the end of the Old Loggers Path—not too far to go!	1.5
26.74	Turn back and forth on several switchbacks that descend adjacent to a small tributary to North Pleasant Stream. This tributary begins where the privately held quarry is located. The trail finally levels along an old logging grade. Highlights of this area include beautiful rock formations and spring flowers.	1.1
27.24	At a very large campsite, the trail turns to the right. Straight ahead, the logging grade leads to a steep drop off which used to cross Hoghouse Run via bridge. The path now skirts around and across the waterway before finding the grade again on the opposite side.	0.60
27.40	The trail takes two quick turns and descends to one last logging grade.	0.44
27.61	A perpetually wet trail is reinforced with the 'corduroy trail' method. A corduroy trail involves logs placed perpendicular to the tread way so that the hiker can stay dry while walking above the muddy trail. Begin the final descent!	0.23
27.78	After the steep descent the trail reaches a gravel road, Masten Road. You are back to the beginning!	0.06

MI Clockwise	TRAIL DESCRIPTION	MI Counter Clockwise
27.84	The Old Loggers Path ends at the beginning of the bridge, right back where it started. To the right is the official parking area, backpacking campsite, restrooms, and car camping sites (reservations required, 570.946.4049).	0.0

NOTEWORTHY SIDE TRAILS

Official blazed trails with forgotten grades and unmaintained trails abound along the OLP. Numerous loops of varying lengths can be created, so for those who are comfortable and prepared to ramble through the woods and get off the main path, enjoy! Below is a list of noteworthy and more popular side trails.

DOE RUN TRAIL

This trail leads upstream away from the Doe Run Shelter at mile 17.59 towards Ellenton Grade. You can create multiple OLP loops and cutoffs with this trail. One scenic day hike loop incorporates Doe Run Trail, Ellenton Grade, OLP and Yellow Dog Road for a gentle 4-mile hike. You will find an excellent vista, beautiful stream and camp along Doe Run, and a fun grassy double-track along a marsh with some amazing wetland plant species.

SUSQUEHANNA AND NEW YORK RAILROAD TRAIL

This old grade on the south side of Pleasant Stream is a great cutoff option for those looking to hike the southern half of OLP. It can also be used for times when Pleasant Stream is too high to cross. It follows along the southside of Pleasant Stream for roughly 3 miles, between Mill Creek Road near Masten and mile 10.24. Although this trail was blazed yellow and maintained in 2024, there are no guarantees on the condition. This trail can be used to create several loops with other surrounding trails. Two listed below:

- **7-mile loop:** From Masten, connect S & NY RR Trail with a 3-mile road walk on Pleasant Stream Road for a 7-mile loop around the stream. You will have to cross Pleasant Stream, so this is not a good option during high water.

- **14-mile loop:** From Masten, use the S & NY RR Trail to create a loop with the southern half of the OLP. This is a great one-day or two-day trip.

SPROUT POINT

A quarter-mile spur off the OLP at mile 4.23. Follow the unnamed gravel double-track road left, which leads to Sprout Point. Sprout Point is the site of an old forest fire tower and stone building. The fire tower is long gone.

SPROUT POINT VISTA:

Definitely stop here. It's a yellow blazed side trail at mile 4.83 that leads 0.1 miles to Sprout Point Vista and a three-sided trail shelter. The shelter is an 'Adirondack' shelter—similar to those found on the Appalachian Trail. Sprout Point Vista provides a great view south to many valleys and ridges, and the nearby shelter provides room to sleep for 6 to 8 hikers. There is also enough room in this area for two tents. Water can be found along the headwaters of East Branch Wallis Run, just off the main OLP in the drainage near the trail. Here, the stream is seasonal at best; hikers may have to walk downstream to find adequate water. Cell service has been reported here.

LONG RUN TRAIL:

This is an unblazed trail that connects OLP with Cherry Ridge Trail. It is maintained but unblazed and sometimes difficult to find.

SHARP SHINNED TRAIL:

This is an old Nordic ski trail that meets the OLP twice within mile 24. You may or may not notice both termini of the Sharp Shinned Trail as you hike along the OLP. It's a fading, yellow-blazed 4-mile loop trail, which leads downstream to Rock Run, connects with Hawkeye Ski Trail on the north side of Rock Run, and then climbs back up to the OLP. It is a gentle trail and when clear, is good for skiing.

SHORT RUN

Like Long Run Trail, this is an unblazed trail that connects OLP with Cherry Ridge Trail. It is maintained, but unblazed and sometimes difficult to find.

CHERRY RIDGE TRAIL

A blue blazed-loop trail at OLP mile 25.76. It begins at the parking area on Krimm Road. It's a 5.7-mile loop that runs in conjunction with the OLP for a short time and remains on the plateau to skirt above Long Run, Short Run, and Bovier Run.

UNNAMED TRAIL ALONG ROCK RUN

Access this trail, sometimes referred to as Yellow Dog Falls Shortcut Trail, from the parking area near the intersection of Rock Run Road and Yellow Dog Road. It leads less than one-half mile to the OLP mile 21.33 at Rock Run, the most popular spot along the whole trail.

YELLOW DOG TRAIL

A short side trail that connects mile 20.03 and Ellenton Ridge Road. It may or may not be blazed, but you'll notice it making a hard right, where the OLP heads left downstream toward Rock Run, to lead south and back to Ellenton Ridge Road. It is an old grade and leads past a marshy area with plenty of great wetland plant species.

For an online map of the Old Loggers Path,
visit Keystone Trails Association at:

www.kta-hike.org/maps

or scan here:

ABOUT THE AUTHOR

Dave has been active in the outdoors his entire life, pursuing several different recreational avenues, with his favorite being long distance hiking. Dave has completed several 'thru hikes' of long distance trails throughout the country along with many of the forest trails that are available in Pennsylvania. Dave's main goal in his work is to introduce and reconnect enthusiasts with the natural world. His goal for this guidebook is to offer an accurate description of the trails so that more people will feel comfortable exploring and protecting this area. You can find more information regarding Dave at his backpacking website: walkwithgantz.weebly.com